Fun for Us

By Madeline Boskey

Target Skill Setting

Scott Foresman
is an imprint of

Glenview, Illinois • Boston, Massachusetts • Chandler, Arizona •
Upper Saddle River, New Jersey

I am Meg.

I can sit with Rick.

I am Meg.

I can mix with Max.

I am Meg.

I can jump with Zack.

I am Meg.

I can tap with Rex.

I am Meg.

I can spin with Nick.

I am Meg.

I can cut with Jack.

I am Meg

I can nap on the mat.